TODAY'S SPORTS GREATS

SIDNEY CROSBY

By Greg Roza

Gareth Stevens
Publishing

Please visit our website, www.garethstevens.com. For a free color catalog of all our high-quality books, call toll free 1-800-542-2595 or fax 1-877-542-2596.

Library of Congress Cataloging-in-Publication Data

Roza, Greg.
Sidney Crosby / Greg Roza.
    p. cm. — (Today's sports greats)
Includes index.
ISBN 978-1-4339-5876-2 (pbk.)
ISBN 978-1-4339-5877-9 (6-pack)
ISBN 978-1-4339-5874-8 (library binding)
1. Crosby, Sidney, 1987—Juvenile literature. 2. Hockey players—Canada—Biography—Juvenile literature. I. Title.
GV848.5.C76R69 2011
796.962092—dc22
[B]

                               2011003856

First Edition

Published in 2012 by
Gareth Stevens Publishing
111 East 14th Street, Suite 349
New York, NY 10003

Copyright © 2012 Gareth Stevens Publishing

Designer: Michael J. Flynn
Editor: Therese Shea

Photo credits: Cover, pp. 1, 23 Gregory Shamus/National Hockey League/Getty Images; p. 4 Gregory Shamus/Getty Images; p. 5 Mike Powell/Getty Images; p. 6 J. Kolis/ Bruce Bennett/Getty Images; p. 8 Dave Sandford/National Hockey League/Getty Images; p. 9 iStockphoto; pp. 11, 14–15 Dave Sandford/Getty Images; p. 12 P. McCallum/ Bruce Bennett/Getty Images; p. 16 Andre Ringuette/Getty Images; pp. 17, 18–19, 29 Bruce Bennett/Getty Images; p. 20 Graig Abel/Getty Images; p. 25 David E. Klutho/ Sports Illustrated/Getty Images; p. 27 Yuri Kadobnov/AFP/Getty Images.

Printed in the United States of America

CPSIA compliance information: Batch #CS11GS: For further information contact Gareth Stevens, New York, New York at 1-800-542-2595.

CONTENTS

Words in the glossary appear in **bold** type the first time they are used in the text.

In 2005, at the age of 18, Sidney "The Kid" Crosby entered the National Hockey League (NHL). Many fans expected him to be one of the greatest athletes to play the game. In a few short years, Crosby proved them right! It took him just 4 years to win the **Stanley Cup**. He was the youngest team captain ever to earn that honor.

Crosby proudly holds the puck he used to score his first NHL goal on October 8, 2005.

Crosby has been a competitor all his life. He was wowing fans by age 7 and has won numerous hockey awards over the years. He's also had the guidance of several hockey stars, including one of the greatest—Mario Lemieux. All this has added up to one of the most exciting careers in professional hockey.

The Nicknames

Many players don't play in the NHL full-time until they're in their early to mid-20s. Crosby earned the nickname "Sid the Kid" because he was younger than most **rookies**. He's also been called "The Next One." This is meant to compare him to Wayne Gretzky, believed by many to be the greatest hockey player of all time. Gretzky earned the nickname "The Great One" during his NHL career.

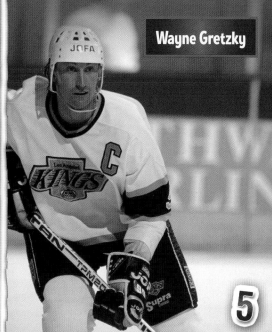

Wayne Gretzky

DID YOU KNOW?

Crosby is a center. This means he plays between two players called wings (or wingers). Centers need to be good at scoring.

Crosby comes from the Canadian province, or region, of Nova Scotia. He was born in the city of Halifax on August 7, 1987, and grew up in Cole Harbour. Crosby became interested in playing hockey at a very early age. Some stories say that at 2 years old, he was playing hockey in the basement of his house and putting dents in the family's clothes dryer!

Crosby is shown here playing for Team Canada in the 2003 Under-18 Junior World Cup.

Crosby was following in the footsteps of his father, Troy Crosby. Troy had played goalie for a junior league hockey team in Quebec, Canada. He had also been **drafted** by the Montreal Canadiens, although he never actually played in the NHL. Troy passed on his love for the game to his son. It wasn't long before Crosby was playing pond hockey with his friends.

What's Pond Hockey?

Pond hockey is played on the frozen surface of a pond or lake. Unlike professional hockey, pond hockey is played with no walls to stop the puck. It's often played without goalies and with goals just a little bit taller than the puck. Sometimes players use a pair of shoes to mark the goal! Many professional players from Canada and the United States got their start playing pond hockey.

DID YOU KNOW?

Growing up, Crosby's favorite hockey player was the Detroit Red Wings' Steve Yzerman. Crosby said, "I really liked the way he played and the way he handled himself."

Sidney poses with his sister, Taylor; mother, Trina; and father, Troy, before the 2011 Winter Classic in Pittsburgh, Pennsylvania.

Troy Crosby quickly noticed that Sidney was a natural at shooting a puck. He took his 2-year-old son to a local ice rink and taught him how to skate. By the time Sidney was 5, he was good enough to join a youth hockey league in Cole Harbour. This was the start of a very successful career.

Hockey Gear

What do you need to play hockey? Just like the young Crosby, all players really need to get started are skates, a stick, and a puck (a tennis ball will work, too). However, anyone interested in playing competitive hockey will need protective gear. This includes a helmet (which may have a cage for the face), mouth guard, gloves, and pads for the shoulders, elbows, chest, and legs. Goalies require special equipment to guard the net.

Sidney's parents supported him as he grew into a talented hockey player. His mother, Trina, took extra jobs to help buy him the equipment he needed. Crosby met with great success in numerous hockey camps. When Sidney was 7, he was interviewed by a local newspaper. Soon, hockey fans across Canada were hearing about a young **phenom** from Cole Harbour named Sidney Crosby.

TEEN HOCKEY STAR

Crosby continued to amaze hockey fans all over Canada. When he was 14, he played for the Dartmouth Subways with boys 3 years older than himself. He was one of the best players in the league, scoring 95 goals in 74 games.

When Crosby was 15, he wanted to play major junior hockey for the Halifax Mooseheads, but he was still too young. Instead, he chose to attend Shattuck-St. Mary's School (SSM) in Faribault, Minnesota. The school was known as one of the best US schools for hockey instruction. During the one season that Crosby played for the SSM Sabres, he scored 72 goals in 57 games. Crosby led the Sabres to a national championship in 2003.

DID YOU KNOW?

Crosby and Jack Johnson were the youngest—and most talented—players on the SSM Sabres. They also played on the SSM baseball team.

Crosby poses with his friend Jack Johnson during the 2005 NHL Draft. Johnson was chosen third by the Carolina Hurricanes.

Jack Johnson

One of Crosby's closest friends and teammates at SSM was current NHL **defenseman** Jack Johnson. Johnson, originally from Indianapolis, Indiana, later played hockey for the University of Michigan Wolverines. He set a freshman record for defensive scoring with 32 points in 38 games. He also helped the US hockey team win a silver medal at the 2010 Olympic Games. Today, Johnson plays professional hockey for the Los Angeles Kings.

Crosby looks to score for the Rimouski Océanic against the Gatineau Olympiques in Gatineau, Quebec, in 2004.

In 2003, Crosby made a big step forward by playing in the Quebec Major Junior Hockey League (QMJHL). He was selected first in the draft by the Rimouski Océanic. At just 16 years old, Crosby played in 59 games for the team. He scored 54 goals and 81 **assists** for a total of 135 points. He also won six major QMJHL awards, including Rookie of the Year, Most Valuable Player (MVP), Personality of the Year, and Top Scorer of the Year.

Crosby was the only player under 18 asked to join Team Canada for the 2004 World Junior Championships. He became the youngest player ever to score a goal in that event. Although Canada lost to the United States in the finals, Crosby helped the team win the silver medal.

The Juniors

Junior hockey leagues in the United States and Canada are similar to the minor leagues in baseball. Junior hockey—often just called "the juniors"—gives young players between the ages of 16 and 20 a chance to improve their skills and prepare for a professional hockey career. There are many junior leagues across North America. The majority of players in the NHL today played in the juniors first.

DID YOU KNOW?

In one game with the Rimouski Océanic, Crosby scored 8 points. In another, he scored a goal from behind the net!

For the 2003–2004 season, Crosby was a superstar for both the Rimouski Océanic and Team Canada. Most hockey fans would say that this is a great feat for a 16-year-old, but Crosby had even more to offer. In the 2004–2005 QMJHL season, he scored 66 goals and 102 assists in 62 games. Once again, Crosby was MVP of the league. The Rimouski Océanic won the QMJHL championship, but lost to the London Knights in the Memorial Cup finals.

Crosby was again selected to play for Team Canada in the 2005 World Junior Championships. This time, Crosby scored six goals and three assists. Team Canada beat Russia to become the 2005 World Junior champions. With one assist in the final game, Crosby said, "This was a dream come true."

Patrice Bergeron (left), Crosby, and Corey perry (right) celebrate Team Canada's gold medal at the 2005 World Junior Championships. Canada defeated Russia 6-1.

Dropping the Gloves

Crosby became a tough player while he was perfecting his stick-handling skills. During his first year in the NHL, he was the first rookie to earn more than 100 points and 100 penalty minutes. About fighting in the juniors, Crosby said, "It is the first time you're seeing your friends get in fights. . . . But once you kind of get past those first couple, you just get used to it. It's part of the game."

DID YOU KNOW?

The Memorial Cup is a contest held each year between the team that hosts the tournament and the top three teams in each of the major junior hockey leagues in the Canadian Hockey League (including the QMJHL).

In 2004–2005, a disagreement between NHL owners and players resulted in a year without professional hockey. Owners, players, and fans alike were especially excited about the 2005 draft, and most people believed Crosby would be selected first overall. In fact, some people were calling the draft the "Sidney Crosby **Sweepstakes**." The Pittsburgh Penguins proved them right by selecting Crosby first.

Hockey great Mario Lemieux was instrumental in getting Crosby to play for the Pittsburgh Penguins.

Crosby signed a 3-year deal with the Penguins for $850,000 a year. This was the most a rookie could make based on an agreement between team owners and players. He was promised more money if he performed well. Crosby also picked up millions of dollars in **endorsement** deals with big-name companies such as Reebok and Gatorade.

The Hockey Lockout

Before the 2004–2005 NHL season, team owners wanted to put a limit on the money they paid players. Players thought that this was unfair. When the two sides couldn't come to an agreement, league **commissioner** Gary Bettman called for a lockout. They finally came to an agreement 310 days later. Due to the lockout, however, there was no 2004–2005 hockey season.

DID YOU KNOW?

A lockout occurs when the owner of a business refuses to let the employees work. This is different from a strike, which is when workers refuse to work.

Gary Bettman

Crosby was under a lot of pressure to do well in his rookie season. He was fortunate to have one of hockey's greatest stars ever—Mario Lemieux—to guide him. Crosby learned about leadership from the team captain. However, Lemieux was forced to retire halfway through the season due to an irregular heartbeat. Crosby was named the **alternate captain**, an honor rarely given to a rookie.

Crosby had an amazing rookie season with the Penguins. In 81 games, he scored 39 goals and 63 assists. However, the Pens won just 22 games and failed to make the **playoffs**. Despite being the second-worst team in the NHL, the Penguins were about to turn things around with the help of Sidney Crosby.

Crosby celebrates his 100th NHL point on April 17, 2006, at Mellon Arena in Pittsburgh.

Life with Lemieux

Even after Lemieux—who was part owner of the Penguins—was forced to retire, he continued to encourage and **mentor** Crosby. Crosby lived with the Lemieux family in Pittsburgh and got to know them very well. He soon felt like part of the family. Crosby continued to live with the Lemieuxs until 2010, when he bought his own home.

DID YOU KNOW?

In April 2006, during a game against the New York Islanders, Crosby became the youngest player ever to reach 100 points.

For the 2006–2007 season, the Penguins added more talent to the team, including two promising young players named Evgeni Malkin and Jordan Staal. By December 2006, Crosby had become the league points leader.

Crosby poses with the Hart Memorial Trophy (left), the Art Ross Trophy (center), and the Lester B. Pearson Award (right) at the 2007 NHL Awards.

For the first time in five seasons, the Pittsburgh Penguins made the playoffs. Crosby finished the regular season with 39 goals and 84 assists for a total of 120 points. These numbers made him the league's leading scorer and earned him the Art Ross Trophy. He became the youngest player ever to win the Hart Memorial Trophy, given to the league MVP. He also won the Lester B. Pearson Award (now called the Ted Lindsay Award), which is given to the most outstanding player as judged by other players in the league.

Crosby Has Hart

Crosby is in good company as a winner of the Hart Memorial Trophy. Since 1924, it has been given each year to the player believed to be most valuable to his team. Other winners include Eddie Shore (four times), Gordie Howe (six times), Bobby Orr (three times), Bobby Clarke (three times), Mario Lemieux (three times), Dominik Hasek (two times), and Alex Ovechkin (two times). Wayne Gretzky has won the award a record nine times.

DID YOU KNOW?

Crosby scored his first hat trick (three goals in one game) on October 28, 2006, when the Penguins defeated the Philadelphia Flyers 8-2.

Before the 2007–2008 season, Crosby experienced two career-changing events. First, he became the Penguins captain—the youngest player in NHL history to receive this honor. Second, he signed a 5-year contract worth $43.5 million!

Unfortunately, partway through the season, Crosby missed 28 games due to an ankle injury. However, Evgeni Malkin stepped up and kept the team playing strong. The Penguins finished the regular season first in their **division** with Crosby back in the lineup. It was back to the playoffs! The Pens battled their way past the Ottawa Senators, New York Rangers, and Philadelphia Flyers, only to lose to the Detroit Red Wings in the Stanley Cup finals. The Pens had come a long way, and the loss was especially difficult.

DID YOU KNOW?

On September 4, 2008, Crosby became the youngest person to receive the Order of Nova Scotia. This award "encourages excellence by recognizing Nova Scotians for outstanding contributions or achievements."

The Winter Classic

On January 1, 2008, the Pittsburgh Penguins played the Buffalo Sabres in the first-ever Winter Classic, which was played the old-fashioned way—outdoors! It was a snowy day in Buffalo, New York, and a very close game. After an exciting afternoon, it was Crosby who scored the game-winning goal during a **shootout**. The Pens won 2–1. The NHL Winter Classic is now an annual event.

Crosby celebrates after his game-winning shootout goal at the 2008 NHL Winter Classic.

For the 2008–2009 season, Crosby, Malkin, and the rest of the Pens got off to a slow start. Many people blamed their defensive-minded coach, Michel Therrien. However, Dan Bylsma replaced Therrien midseason. Soon, the team turned back into a scoring machine. The Pens made the playoffs for the third straight year.

After taking out the Philadelphia Flyers, Washington Capitals, and Carolina Hurricanes, the Penguins once again faced the Detroit Red Wings in the Stanley Cup finals. The Red Wings were looking for back-to-back championships, but Crosby had another plan. After trailing two games to none, the Pens rallied to win the series in seven games. They were finally champions, with Crosby as the youngest team captain ever to win the Stanley Cup.

DID YOU KNOW?

During the Stanley Cup playoffs, Crosby received a new endorsement deal from Reebok. It was the largest deal ever signed by a professional hockey player.

As team captain, Crosby was the first player to lift the Stanley Cup above his head.

What's the Stanley Cup?

The NHL postseason is called the Stanley Cup playoffs. The name comes from the award given to the winner—a "cup" made of silver and nickel that weighs 34.5 pounds (15.6 kg) and is 35.25 inches (89.5 cm) tall. Each year, the names of the players on the winning team are engraved on the cup. That team keeps the award for 100 days. Lifting the cup above your head is a symbol of victory. It's the greatest accomplishment a professional hockey player can achieve.

Although the Penguins were knocked out of the 2010 playoffs by the Montreal Canadiens, Crosby had another award-winning season. He received his first Maurice "Rocket" Richard Trophy for leading the league in goals with 51. He also won the Mark Messier Leadership Award, given to a player "in recognition of his commitment and service to charities in his community."

Perhaps the most impressive award Crosby won that season didn't have anything to do with the NHL. For the first time, Crosby was chosen to play for Team Canada in the 2010 Winter Olympics. Once again, Crosby came up big. In the final round, his overtime goal against the US team earned him and Team Canada the gold medal.

DID YOU KNOW?

The game-winning puck from the 2010 Olympics is in the Hockey Hall of Fame in Toronto, Canada.

The Case of the Missing Gloves

Upon scoring the winning goal at the 2010 Olympics, Crosby tossed his stick and gloves into the air in celebration. Later, it was discovered the equipment was missing. Some believed it had been stolen. This bothered many people, who wanted the gloves and stick to be placed in the Hockey Hall of Fame in Canada. Reebok even offered a $10,000 reward! It turned out the equipment had been packed into another player's bag by mistake.

SPEAK SOFTLY, CARRY A BIG HOCKEY STICK

In December 2010, the Canadian Press named Crosby male athlete of the year by giving him the Lionel Conacher Award. This was the third time Crosby had won the award. Many fans think that it's just a matter of time before he lifts the Stanley Cup above his head once again.

On the ice, Crosby is a dynamic leader with amazing skills. Off the ice, he's soft-spoken and humble. But his desire to improve as a player and his determination to win remain strong wherever he is.

"I'm not trying to be the next Wayne Gretzky or Mario Lemieux," Crosby once said. "I am putting pressure on myself to do my best and perform to my **potential**; that's all I can do."

DID YOU KNOW?

Crosby has appeared in several movies. Most of them are about hockey. He played himself in the 2010 movie *She's Out of My League*.

Crosby's Award-Winning Career

Crosby has won dozens of awards over the years. Here's a list of the most impressive.

Quebec Major Junior Hockey League (QMJHL)
Rookie of the Year – 2004
Michel Briere Trophy (league MVP) – 2004, 2005
Jean Béliveau Trophy (leading scorer) – 2004, 2005
Guy Lafleur Trophy (playoff MVP) – 2005
Canadian Hockey League
Leading Scorer – 2004, 2005
Player of the Year – 2004, 2005
Rookie of the Year – 2004
Ed Chynoweth Trophy (Memorial Cup leading scorer) – 2005
National Hockey League
Maurice "Rocket" Richard Trophy (most goals) – 2010
Mark Messier Leadership Award – 2010, 2007
Stanley Cup Championship – 2009
Hart Memorial Trophy (league MVP) – 2007
Lester B. Pearson Award (now Ted Lindsay Award) (outstanding player as voted by other players) – 2007
Art Ross Award (leading scorer) – 2007
International Hockey
Olympic Ice Hockey Gold Medal – 2010
Ice Hockey World Championships Leading Scorer – 2006
Ice Hockey World Championships Best Forward – 2006
World Junior Championships Gold Medal – 2005
World Junior Championships Silver Medal – 2004
Other
Order of Nova Scotia – 2008
Lionel Conacher Award (male athlete of the year) – 2007, 2009, 2010

GLOSSARY

alternate captain: a player chosen to lead the team if the captain is injured

assist: a point awarded to a player who passes the puck to a player who scores

commissioner: the leader of a group or organization

defenseman: a player skilled at stopping other players from scoring

division: a group of teams located near each other within a league

draft: to select to play for a team. Also, the selection of new players for a team.

endorsement: the act of supporting a product, especially for money

mentor: to provide advice and support to a less experienced person

phenom: a remarkable or outstanding person. It comes from the word *phenomenon*.

playoffs: a series of games that decide a championship

potential: the possibility of succeeding

rookie: a player who is in the first year of playing a sport

shootout: a way to settle a tie that involves players taking turns at shooting the puck into the goal

Stanley Cup: the trophy that is awarded to the National Hockey League team that wins the annual championship

sweepstakes: a game of chance with a major prize

FOR MORE INFORMATION

Books

Hollingsworth, Paul. *Sidney Crosby: The Story of a Champion.* Halifax, Nova Scotia, Canada: Nimbus Publishing, 2010.

Labrecque, Ellen. *Pittsburgh Penguins.* Mankato, MN: Child's World, 2011.

Savage, Jeff. *Sidney Crosby.* Minneapolis, MN: Lerner Publications, 2009.

Websites

Crosby87
crosby87.com
Learn more about the hockey superstar on his official website.

Pittsburgh Penguins
penguins.nhl.com
Stay up to date on Pittsburgh Penguin news by visiting their website.

Sidney Crosby
penguins.nhl.com/club/player.htm?id=8471675
Read the latest news and figures about Crosby, or explore links to other hockey players.

INDEX